This
PLANNER
belongs to

School _____

Grade _____

Room _____

Address _____

_____

Email _____

Phone _____

CONTACTS
and Volunteers

Name	Contact Info

WELCOME

Schedule

SCHOOL BEGINS: _____

LUNCH: _____ RECESS: _____

SPECIALS: _____

_____

SCHOOL ENDS: _____

Need Help?

RELIABLE STUDENTS: _____

TEACHERS: _____

PRINCIPAL: _____

VICE PRINCIPAL: _____

OTHER STAFF: _____

Special Schedules

NAME	TIME/LOCATION
_____	_____
_____	_____
_____	_____
_____	_____

Additional Notes

_____

_____

_____

_____

_____

COMMUNICATION
Log

DATE	TYPE	NAME	PURPOSE	NOTES
	📱 @ 📄 👥			
	📱 @ 📄 👥			
	📱 @ 📄 👥			
	📱 @ 📄 👥			
	📱 @ 📄 👥			
	📱 @ 📄 👥			
	📱 @ 📄 👥			
	📱 @ 📄 👥			
	📱 @ 📄 👥			
	📱 @ 📄 👥			
	📱 @ 📄 👥			
	📱 @ 📄 👥			
	📱 @ 📄 👥			
	📱 @ 📄 👥			
	📱 @ 📄 👥			
	📱 @ 📄 👥			
	📱 @ 📄 👥			
	📱 @ 📄 👥			
	📱 @ 📄 👥			
	📱 @ 📄 👥			
	📱 @ 📄 👥			
	📱 @ 📄 👥			
	📱 @ 📄 👥			
	📱 @ 📄 👥			
	📱 @ 📄 👥			
	📱 @ 📄 👥			

COMMUNICATION
Log

DATE	TYPE	NAME	PURPOSE	NOTES
	📱 @ 📋 👥			
	📱 @ 📋 👥			
	📱 @ 📋 👥			
	📱 @ 📋 👥			
	📱 @ 📋 👥			
	📱 @ 📋 👥			
	📱 @ 📋 👥			
	📱 @ 📋 👥			
	📱 @ 📋 👥			
	📱 @ 📋 👥			
	📱 @ 📋 👥			
	📱 @ 📋 👥			
	📱 @ 📋 👥			
	📱 @ 📋 👥			
	📱 @ 📋 👥			
	📱 @ 📋 👥			
	📱 @ 📋 👥			
	📱 @ 📋 👥			
	📱 @ 📋 👥			
	📱 @ 📋 👥			
	📱 @ 📋 👥			
	📱 @ 📋 👥			
	📱 @ 📋 👥			
	📱 @ 📋 👥			
	📱 @ 📋 👥			
	📱 @ 📋 👥			

NEWS and NOTES

NEWS and NOTES

PLAN *it*

Use these pages to create a classroom plan, record seating charts, create checklists, sketch plans, etc. The options are endless!

YEAR at a GLANCE

July

August

September

October

November

December

YEAR at a GLANCE

January

February

March

April

May

June

JULY / Kind vibes, y'all.

SUNDAY	MONDAY	TUESDAY	WEDNESDAY
○	○	○	○
○	○	○	○
○	○	○	○
○	○	○	○
○	○	○	○

THURSDAY	FRIDAY	SATURDAY	Have To Do
○	○	○	○ ___ ○ ___ ○ ___ ○ ___ ○ ___ ○ ___ ○ ___ ○ ___ ○ ___ ○ ___ ○ ___ ○ ___ ○ ___
○	○	○	
○	○	○	Notes
○	○	○	
○	○	○	

PSST! USE THESE GUIDES TO KEEP YOUR TABS PERFECTLY PLACED.

AUGUST / *It's a good day for a good deed.*

SUNDAY	MONDAY	TUESDAY	WEDNESDAY

14

THURSDAY	FRIDAY	SATURDAY	Have To Do
			Notes

SEPTEMBER

A moment of kindness can change a child's life.

SUNDAY	MONDAY	TUESDAY	WEDNESDAY

THURSDAY	FRIDAY	SATURDAY	Have To Do
◯	◯	◯	◯ ____
◯	◯	◯	
◯	◯	◯	**Notes**
◯	◯	◯	
◯	◯	◯	

OCTOBER

SUNDAY	MONDAY	TUESDAY	WEDNESDAY

THURSDAY	FRIDAY	SATURDAY	Have To Do
			○
			○
			○
			Notes

NOVEMBER / Hugs, not ughs!

SUNDAY	MONDAY	TUESDAY	WEDNESDAY
○	○	○	○
○	○	○	○
○	○	○	○
○	○	○	○
○	○	○	○

Goals

THURSDAY	FRIDAY	SATURDAY	Have To Do
◯	◯	◯	◯
◯	◯	◯	◯ ◯ ◯ ◯ ◯ ◯ ◯ ◯ ◯ ◯ ◯
◯	◯	◯	**Notes**
◯	◯	◯	
◯	◯	◯	

DECEMBER

/ *The brightest people help others shine.*

SUNDAY	MONDAY	TUESDAY	WEDNESDAY

THURSDAY	FRIDAY	SATURDAY	Have To Do
			○ ____ ○ ____ ○ ____ ○ ____ ○ ____ ○ ____ ○ ____ ○ ____ ○ ____ ○ ____ ○ ____
			Notes

JANUARY / *Change the world with kindness.*

SUNDAY	MONDAY	TUESDAY	WEDNESDAY
◯	◯	◯	◯
◯	◯	◯	◯
◯	◯	◯	◯
◯	◯	◯	◯
◯	◯	◯	◯

THURSDAY	FRIDAY	SATURDAY	Have To Do
○	○	○	○
○	○	○	○
○	○	○	Notes
○	○	○	
○	○	○	

FEBRUARY / *Kindness is a choice.*

SUNDAY	MONDAY	TUESDAY	WEDNESDAY
○	○	○	○
○	○	○	○
○	○	○	○
○	○	○	○
○	○	○	○

THURSDAY	FRIDAY	SATURDAY	Have To Do
○	○	○	○ _____ ○ _____ ○ _____ ○ _____ ○ _____ ○ _____ ○ _____
○	○	○	○ _____ ○ _____ ○ _____ ○ _____ ○ _____ ○ _____
○	○	○	Notes
○	○	○	
○	○	○	

MARCH / No act of kindness is too small.

SUNDAY	MONDAY	TUESDAY	WEDNESDAY
○	○	○	○
○	○	○	○
○	○	○	○
○	○	○	○
○	○	○	○

THURSDAY	FRIDAY	SATURDAY	Have To Do
○	○	○	○
○	○	○	○
○	○	○	Notes
○	○	○	
○	○	○	

APRIL / See the ability, not the disability.

SUNDAY	MONDAY	TUESDAY	WEDNESDAY
○	○	○	○
○	○	○	○
○	○	○	○
○	○	○	○
○	○	○	○

THURSDAY	FRIDAY	SATURDAY	Have To Do
			○
			○
			○
			○
			○
			○
			○
			○
			○
			○
			○
			Notes

MAY / Do good, be good, feel good.

SUNDAY	MONDAY	TUESDAY	WEDNESDAY
○	○	○	○
○	○	○	○
○	○	○	○
○	○	○	○
○	○	○	○

THURSDAY	FRIDAY	SATURDAY	Have To Do
○	○	○	○
			○
			○
○	○	○	○
			○
			○
○	○	○	**Notes**
○	○	○	
○	○	○	

JUNE / Make kindness your superpower.

SUNDAY	MONDAY	TUESDAY	WEDNESDAY
○	○	○	○
○	○	○	○
○	○	○	○
○	○	○	○
○	○	○	○

Goals

THURSDAY	FRIDAY	SATURDAY	Have To Do
○	○	○	○ ___ ○ ___ ○ ___ ○ ___ ○ ___ ○ ___ ○ ___
○	○	○	○ ___ ○ ___ ○ ___ ○ ___ ○ ___
○	○	○	Notes
○	○	○	
○	○	○	

WEEK#

Subject	Subject	Subject

MON.
/

TUES.
/

WED.
/

THURS.
/

FRI.
/

Subject	Subject	Subject	Subject

PSST! CUT THIS CORNER OFF EACH WEEK TO MARK AND FIND YOUR PLACE EASILY

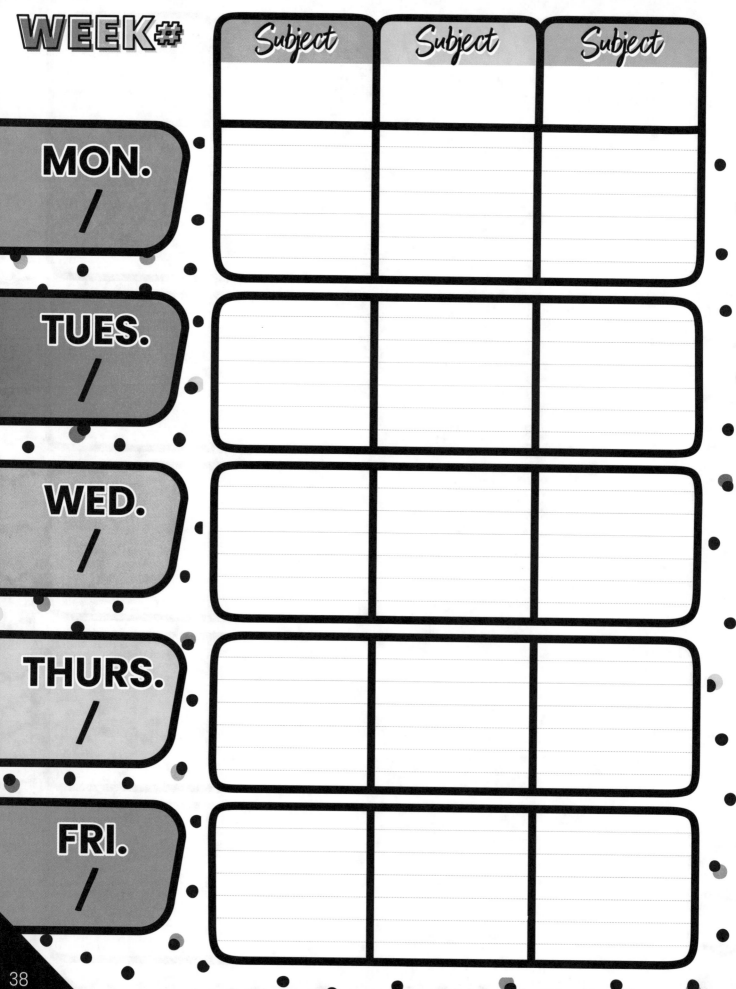

WEEK

Subject	Subject	Subject

MON. /

TUES. /

WED. /

THURS. /

FRI. /

Subject	Subject	Subject	Subject

WEEK#

Subject	Subject	Subject

MON.
/

TUES.
/

WED.
/

THURS.
/

FRI.
/

40

Subject	Subject	Subject	Subject

WEEK

Subject	Subject	Subject

MON. /

TUES. /

WED. /

THURS. /

FRI. /

Subject	Subject	Subject	Subject

43

WEEK#

Subject	Subject	Subject

MON.
/

TUES.
/

WED.
/

THURS.
/

FRI.
/

Subject	Subject	Subject	Subject

WEEK#

Subject	Subject	Subject

MON.
/

TUES.
/

WED.
/

THURS.
/

FRI.
/

Subject	Subject	Subject	Subject

WEEK#

Subject	Subject	Subject

MON.
/

TUES.
/

WED.
/

THURS.
/

FRI.
/

Subject	Subject	Subject	Subject

WEEK#

Subject	Subject	Subject

MON.
/

TUES.
/

WED.
/

THURS.
/

FRI.
/

Subject	Subject	Subject	Subject

WEEK#

Subject	Subject	Subject

MON. /

TUES. /

WED. /

THURS. /

FRI. /

Subject	Subject	Subject	Subject

WEEK#

Subject	Subject	Subject

MON. /

TUES. /

WED. /

THURS. /

FRI. /

54

Subject	Subject	Subject	Subject

WEEK

Subject	Subject	Subject

MON. /

TUES. /

WED. /

THURS. /

FRI. /

Subject	Subject	Subject	Subject

WEEK

Subject	Subject	Subject

MON. /

TUES. /

WED. /

THURS. /

FRI. /

Subject	Subject	Subject	Subject

WEEK

	Subject	Subject	Subject
MON. /			
TUES. /			
WED. /			
THURS. /			
FRI. /			

Subject	Subject	Subject	Subject

WEEK#

Subject	Subject	Subject

MON.
/

TUES.
/

WED.
/

THURS.
/

FRI.
/

Subject	Subject	Subject	Subject

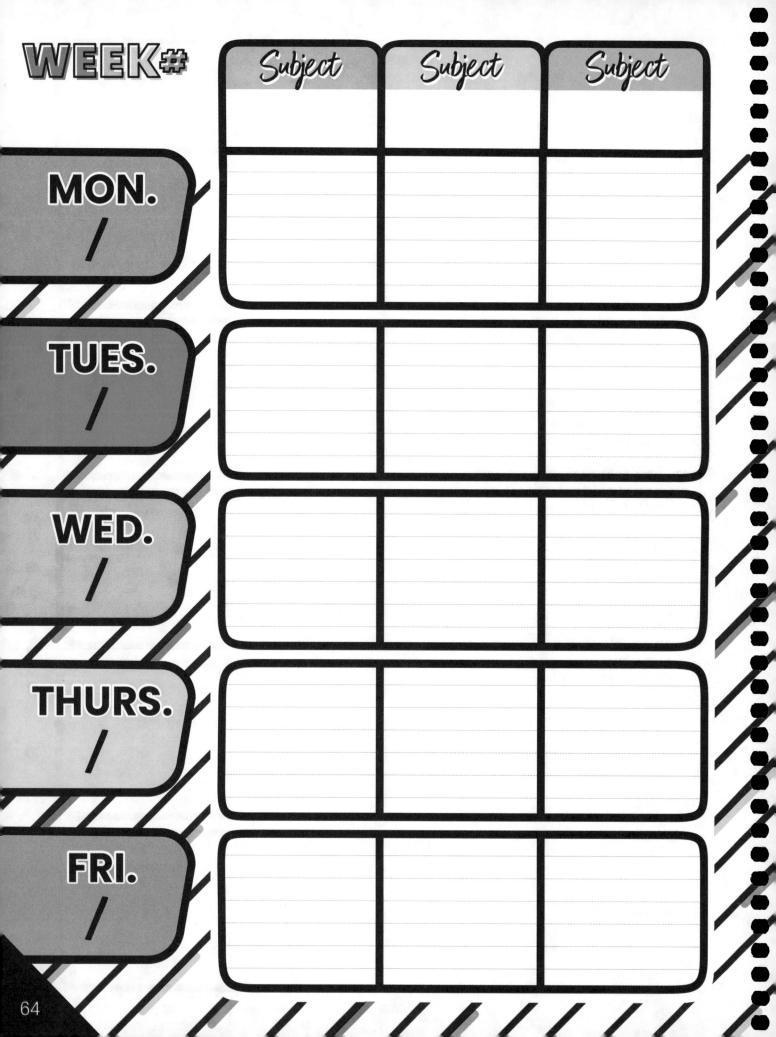

WEEK#

Subject	Subject	Subject

MON. /

TUES. /

WED. /

THURS. /

FRI. /

Subject	Subject	Subject	Subject

WEEK

Subject	Subject	Subject

MON. /

TUES. /

WED. /

THURS. /

FRI. /

Subject	Subject	Subject	Subject

WEEK

Subject	Subject	Subject

MON. /

TUES. /

WED. /

THURS. /

FRI. /

Subject	Subject	Subject	Subject

WEEK#

Subject	Subject	Subject

MON.
/

TUES.
/

WED.
/

THURS.
/

FRI.
/

Subject	Subject	Subject	Subject

71

WEEK#

	Subject	Subject	Subject
MON. /			
TUES. /			
WED. /			
THURS. /			
FRI. /			

Subject	Subject	Subject	Subject

WEEK

	Subject	Subject	Subject
MON. /			
TUES. /			
WED. /			
THURS. /			
FRI. /			

Subject	Subject	Subject	Subject

WEEK

Subject	Subject	Subject

MON.
/

TUES.
/

WED.
/

THURS.
/

FRI.
/

Subject	Subject	Subject	Subject

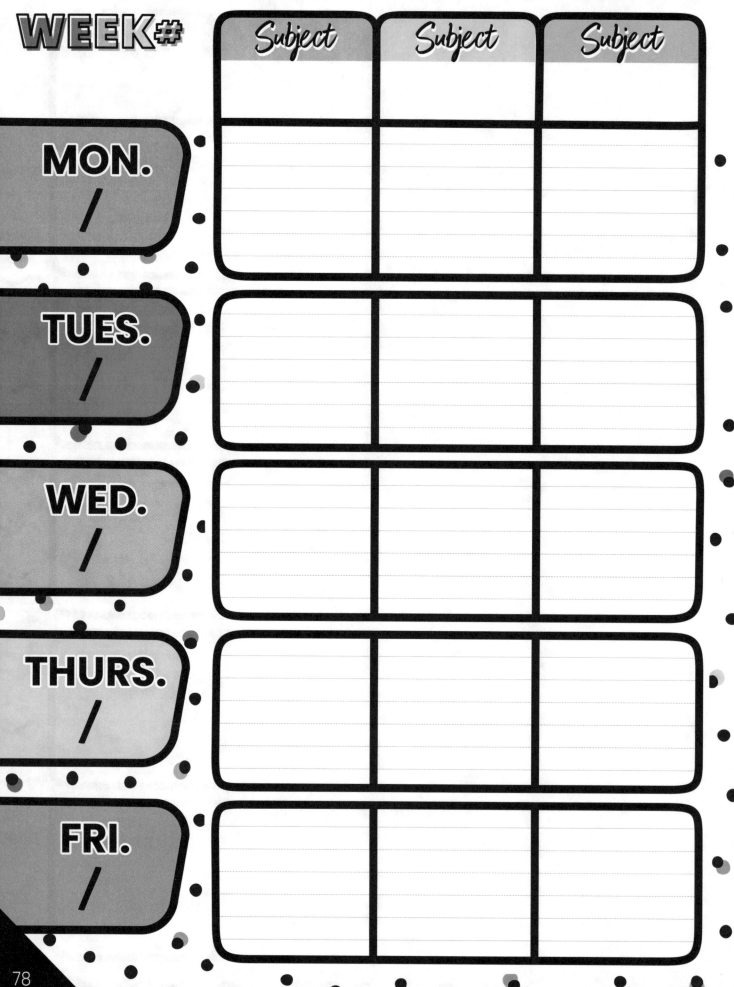

WEEK#

Subject	Subject	Subject

MON.
/

TUES.
/

WED.
/

THURS.
/

FRI.
/

Subject	Subject	Subject	Subject

WEEK

Subject	Subject	Subject

MON.
/

TUES.
/

WED.
/

THURS.
/

FRI.
/

Subject	Subject	Subject	Subject

WEEK#

Subject	Subject	Subject

MON.
/

TUES.
/

WED.
/

THURS.
/

FRI.
/

Subject	Subject	Subject	Subject

WEEK

	Subject	Subject	Subject
MON. /			
TUES. /			
WED. /			
THURS. /			
FRI. /			

Subject	Subject	Subject	Subject

WEEK

Subject	Subject	Subject

MON.
/

TUES.
/

WED.
/

THURS.
/

FRI.
/

Subject	Subject	Subject	Subject

87

WEEK#

Subject	Subject	Subject

MON.
/

TUES.
/

WED.
/

THURS.
/

FRI.
/

Subject	Subject	Subject	Subject

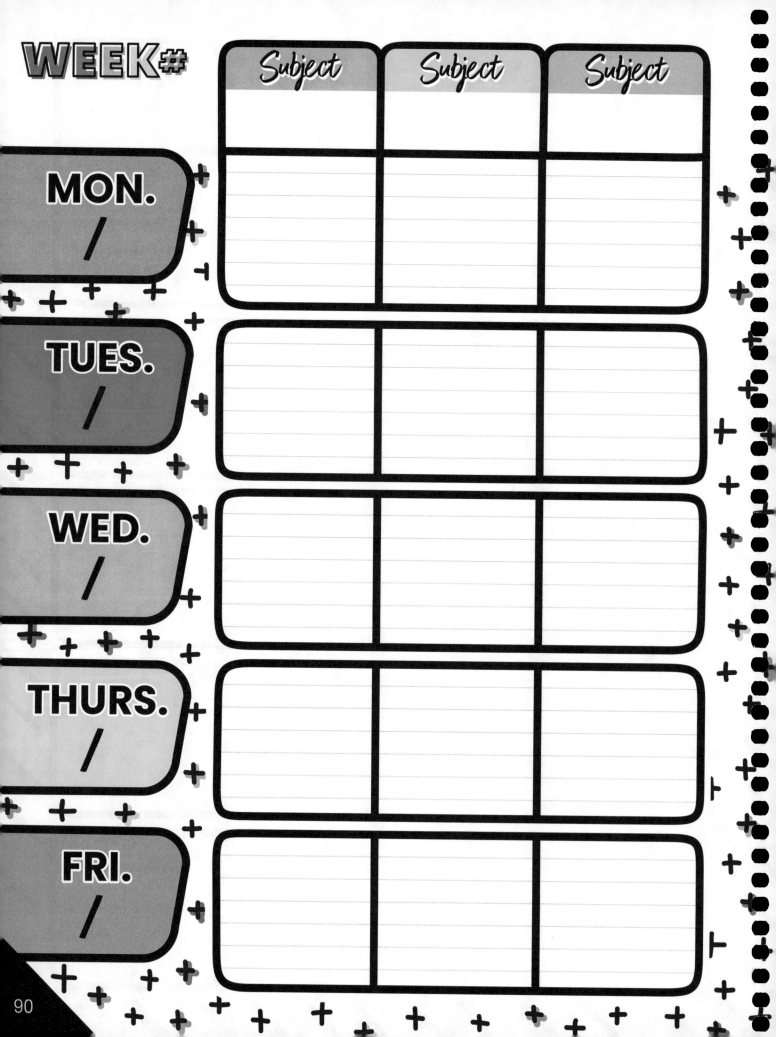

WEEK#

	Subject	*Subject*	*Subject*
MON. /			
TUES. /			
WED. /			
THURS. /			
FRI. /			

Subject	Subject	Subject	Subject

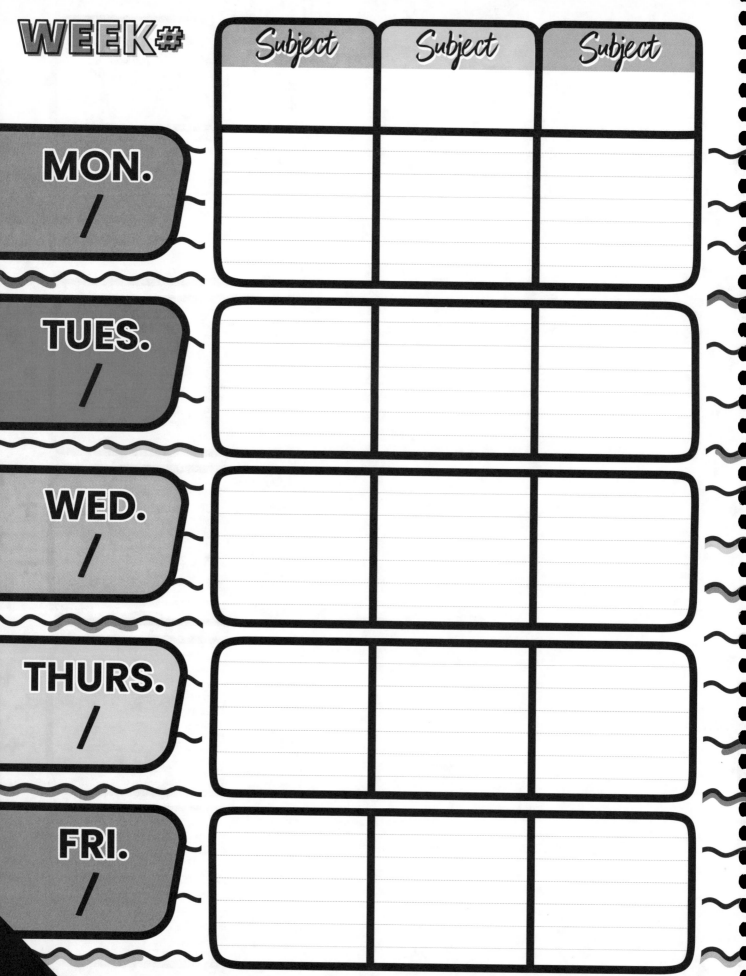

WEEK#

	Subject	Subject	Subject
MON. /			
TUES. /			
WED. /			
THURS. /			
FRI. /			

Subject	Subject	Subject	Subject

WEEK#

Subject	Subject	Subject

MON.
/

TUES.
/

WED.
/

THURS.
/

FRI.
/

Subject	Subject	Subject	Subject

WEEK#

Subject	Subject	Subject

MON.
/

TUES.
/

WED.
/

THURS.
/

FRI.
/

Subject	Subject	Subject	Subject

WEEK

Subject	Subject	Subject

MON. /

TUES. /

WED. /

THURS. /

FRI. /

Subject	Subject	Subject	Subject

WEEK#

	Subject	Subject	Subject
MON. /			
TUES. /			
WED. /			
THURS. /			
FRI. /			

Subject	Subject	Subject	Subject

WEEK#

	Subject	Subject	Subject
MON. /			
TUES. /			
WED. /			
THURS. /			
FRI. /			

WEEK#

Subject	Subject	Subject

MON.
/

TUES.
/

WED.
/

THURS.
/

FRI.
/

Subject	Subject	Subject	Subject

WEEK#

Subject	Subject	Subject

MON.
___/___

TUES.
___/___

WED.
___/___

THURS.
___/___

FRI.
___/___

Subject	Subject	Subject	Subject

WEEK#

Subject	Subject	Subject

MON.
/

TUES.
/

WED.
/

THURS.
/

FRI.
/

Subject	Subject	Subject	Subject

WEEK#

	Subject	Subject	Subject
MON. /			
TUES. /			
WED. /			
THURS. /			
FRI. /			

Subject	Subject	Subject	Subject

WEEK

Subject	Subject	Subject

MON.
/

TUES.
/

WED.
/

THURS.
/

FRI.
/

Subject	Subject	Subject	Subject

WEEK#

Subject	Subject	Subject

MON.
/

TUES.
/

WED.
/

THURS.
/

FRI.
/

Subject	Subject	Subject	Subject

CHECKLIST

Name

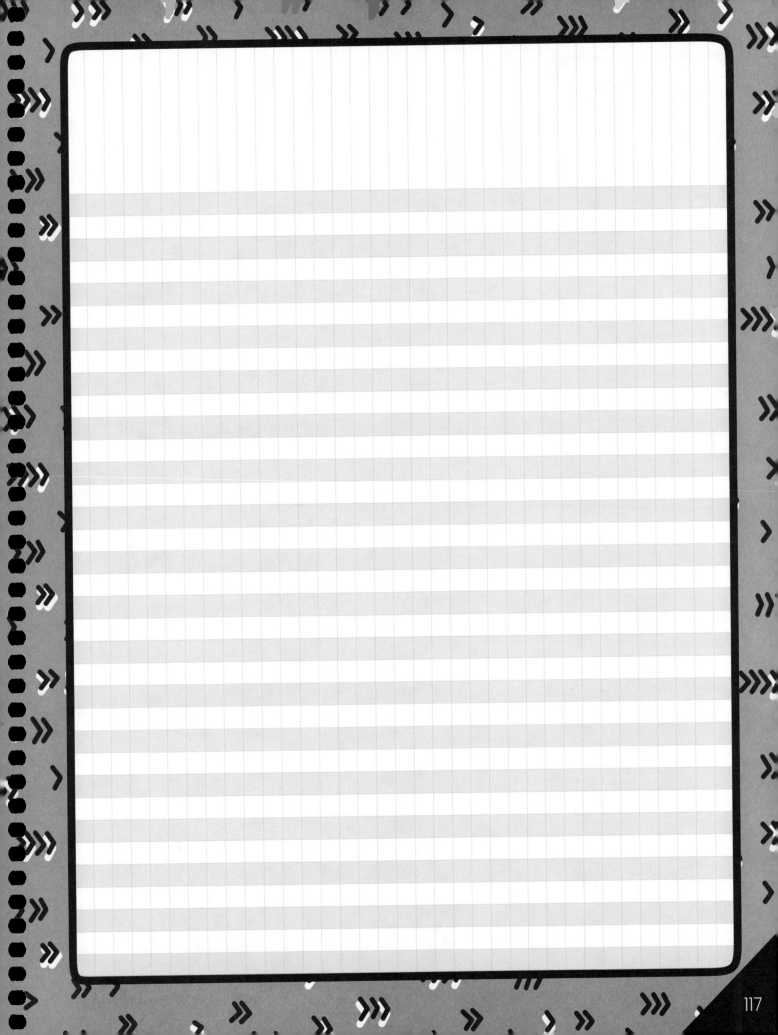

CHECKLIST

Name

PSST! CUT THIS SECTION OFF SO YOU ONLY HAVE TO WRITE YOUR CLASS LIST ONCE.

CHECKLIST

Name

CHECKLIST

Name

CHECKLIST

Name

CHECKLIST

Name

Kindness is **FREE.** Sprinkle that **STUFF** everywhere.

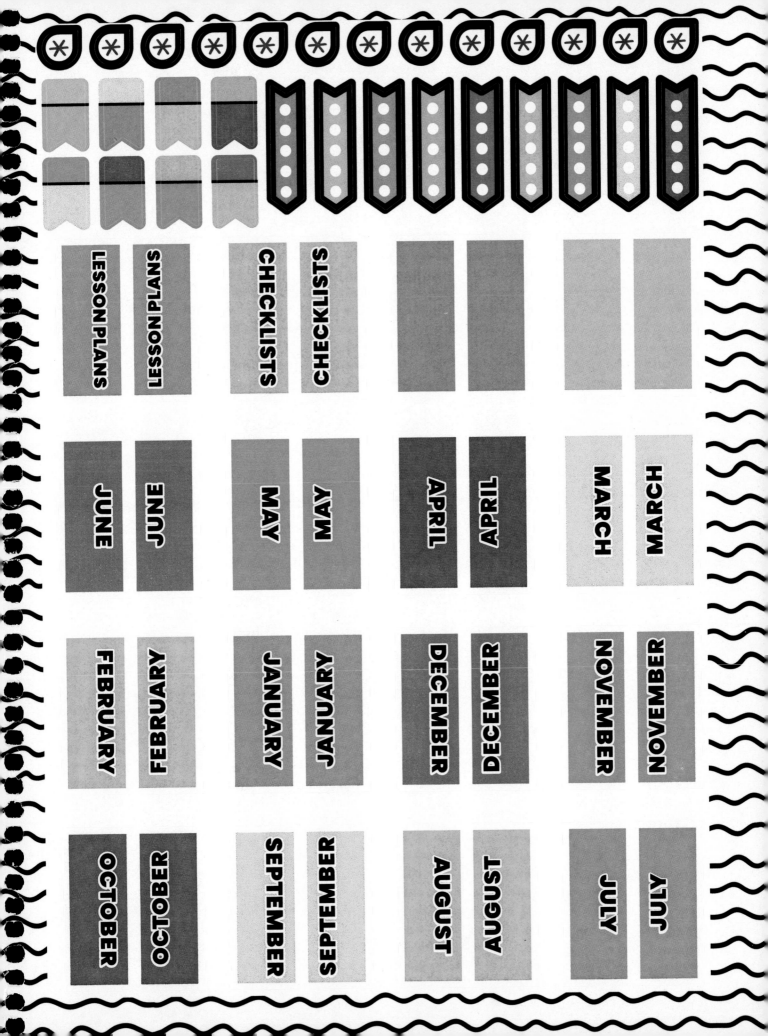

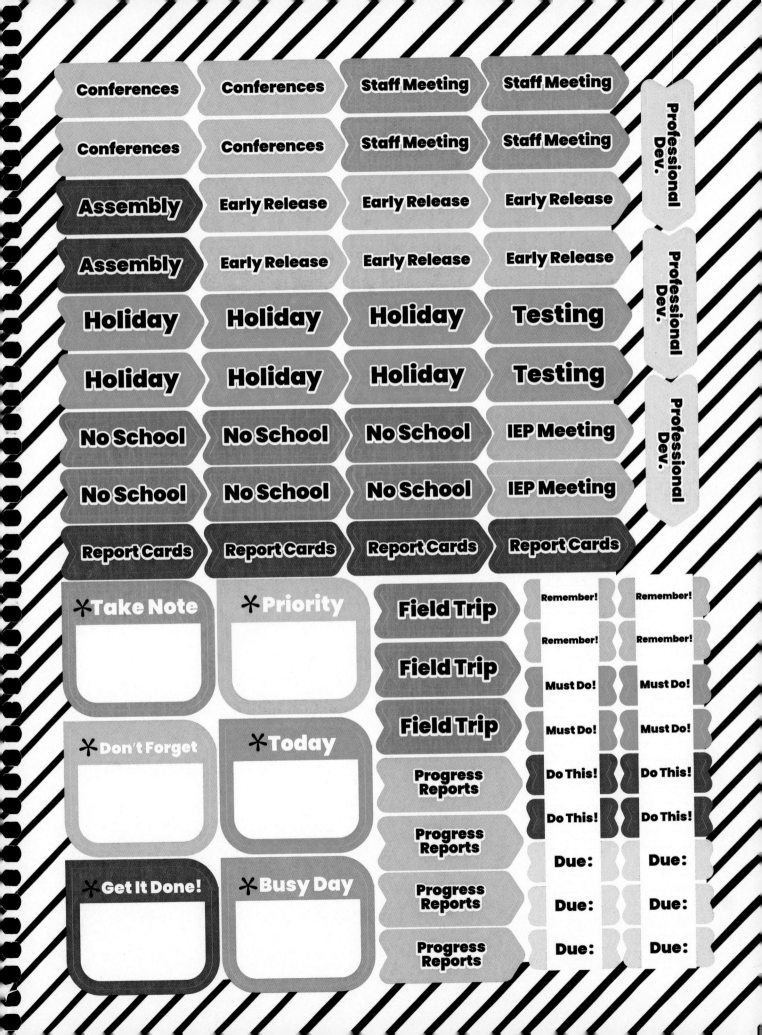